MAPS CHARTS GRAPHS

The Places Around Me

Level A

Sally J. Allen
Writer and Social Studies
Educational Consultant

Sharon M. Marosi
Project Editor

Francyne Abate
Cover Design

Remen-Willis Design Group
Project Design and Illustration

Jerry Harston
Cover Illustration

Modern Curriculum Press
An Imprint of Pearson Learning
299 Jefferson Road, P.O. Box 480
Parsippany, NJ 07054-0480
http://www.mcschool.com

Published simultaneously in Canada by Globe / Modern Curriculum Press, Toronto.

ISBN 0-8136-2132-1   12 13 14 15 16 17 PO   05 04 03 02 01 00 99

Reading a Picture

WHAT I WILL LEARN What is in a picture?
How can I learn from a picture?

Look at this picture. Read the **title**.

FUN AT THE ZOO

CIRCLE IT

1. What does the picture show?

   a zoo   a circus   a farm

2. What are the seals doing?

   sleeping   eating

3. How many children wear red shirts?

   1   2   3

4. Circle a child alone.

5. How many penguins are there?

   2   4   6

6. How many balloons are there?

   2   4   6

COLOR IT

7. Color the balloons green.

8. Color the ice cream cones yellow.

Titles Help Us

WHAT I WILL LEARN What does a picture title do?
What does a map title tell me?

Titles tell what a picture is about.

Here is a picture with a title.

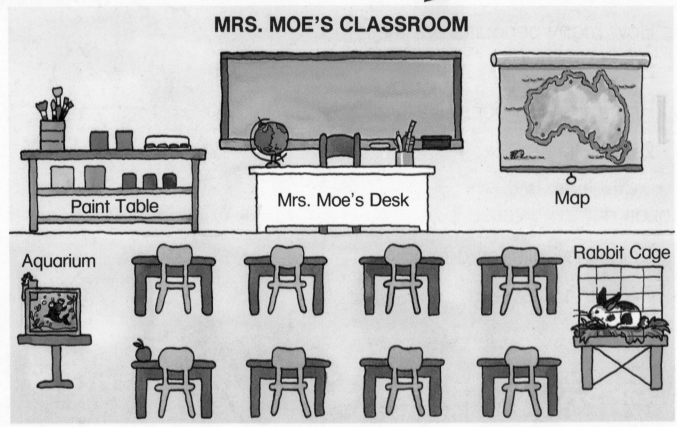

MRS. MOE'S CLASSROOM

Paint Table Mrs. Moe's Desk Map

Aquarium Rabbit Cage

CIRCLE IT

1. What does this picture show?

   a classroom   **a school**   **a playground**

2. Circle the title on the picture.

Titles tell about **maps** too.

Look at this map. Find the title.

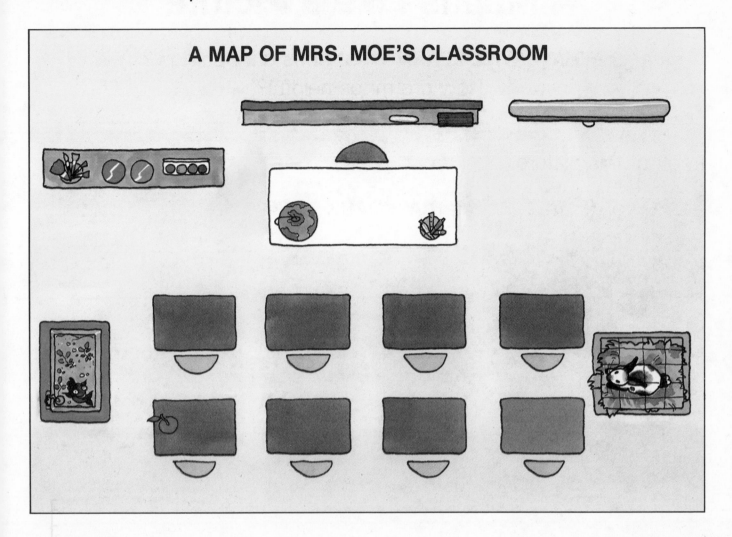

A MAP OF MRS. MOE'S CLASSROOM

CIRCLE IT

3. What does this map show?

   a classroom   **a playground**   **a zoo**

4. Circle the title on the map.

5. Circle the paint table on the map.

COLOR IT

6. Color Mrs. Moe's desk brown.

A Map Is Like a Picture

WHAT I WILL LEARN What does a map show?
How are maps helpful?

Look at this picture.

This picture shows what Maria's back yard looks like.

CIRCLE IT

1. Circle the sandbox in the picture.

2. Find the tree. Circle it.

3. Circle the seesaw.

4. What does this picture show?

   a place   **a person**   **an animal**

A **map** shows what a place looks like. Here is a
map that Maria drew. It shows her back yard.

Maria's map looks like the picture.

But it is different too. It uses drawn pictures
to stand for real things.

Maria took her map to school. She showed her
back yard to her class.

CIRCLE IT

5. Find the tree. Circle it.

6. Circle the sandbox.

7. What does a map show?

   a place   **a person**   **an animal**

Direction Words

WHAT I WILL LEARN What words tell where something is?
Can I match directions with words?

This is a **picture.** It has words on it.
These words tell where things are.

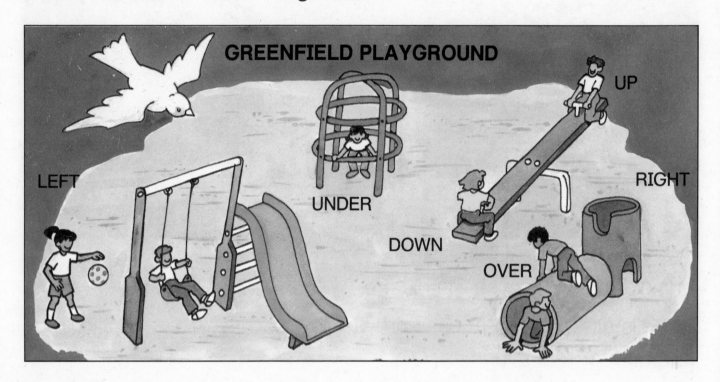

COLOR IT

1. Color the shirt of the child who is UP blue.

2. Color the shirt of the child UNDER the monkey bars red.

3. Color the shirt of the child on the LEFT side of the playground yellow.

4. Color the animal that is OVER the playground brown.

Here is a picture map. It shows Fun Park.

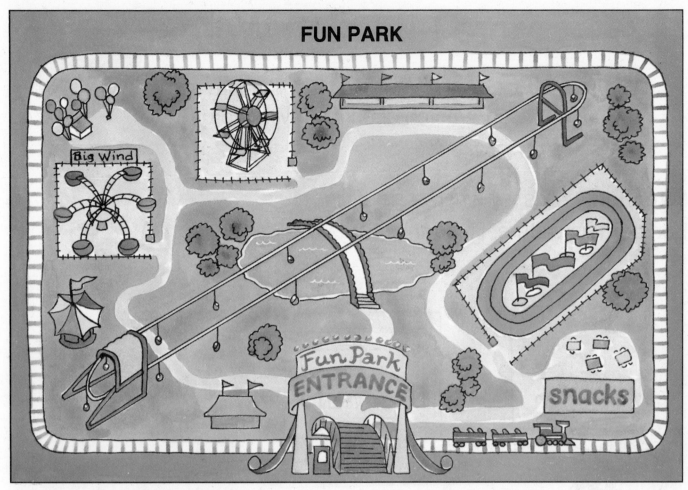

CIRCLE THE RIGHT WORD

Choose the right word. Circle it.

5. The ⚙ is (**left   right**) of the ✴.

6. The ⚙ takes you up and (**under   down**).

7. The Entrance is (**right   left**) of the 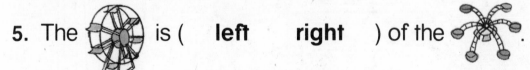.

8. The ⌐ goes (**over   under**) the park.

More Direction Words

WHAT I WILL LEARN What words tell where something is?
Can I match directions with words?

Direction words tell where something is.
Look at this picture. Read the words on it.

TODD'S ROOM

BETWEEN

BACKWARD

FORWARD

TOWARD

AWAY FROM

CIRCLE THE RIGHT WORD

1. The (**turtle**   **bed**) is BETWEEN the ball and the car.

2. Todd's cap is on (**backward**   **forward**).

3. Todd is walking (**away from**   **toward**) the door.

4. Todd's dog is walking TOWARD the (**window**   **bed**).

5. The robot is going (**forward**   **backward**) up the pillow.

CIRCLE IT

6. If Todd walks FORWARD two steps, what will he step on?

7. If Todd walks BACKWARD two steps, what will he step on?

DRAW A LINE

8. Draw a line BETWEEN the red books.

9. Draw a line like this ➡ from the door TOWARD the window.

Finding Cardinal Directions

WHAT I WILL LEARN What are the four directions?
How do I find the directions?

There are four main directions. These are the **cardinal**
directions. They are **North, South, East** and **West.**

THE GLOBE

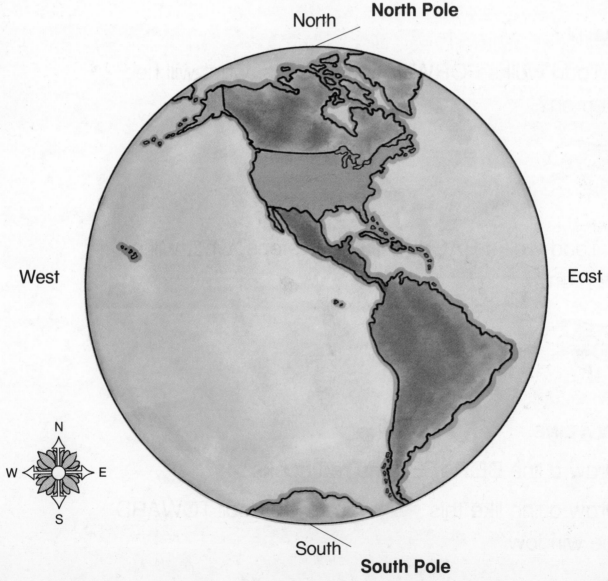

North Pole

North

West

East

South

South Pole

On our earth, North is toward the **North Pole.** South is toward the **South Pole.** Look for the poles on this map.

CIRCLE IT

1. Find the **North Pole** and circle it.

2. Find and circle the **South Pole.**

Face North. East is to the right of North. The sun rises there. West is to the left of North. The sun goes down there.

A **compass** tells us direction on a map. Find the compasses below. North and South are opposites. East and West are opposites.

PRINT IT

3. Here are two compasses. One has been done for you. One has directions missing. Print the missing letters.

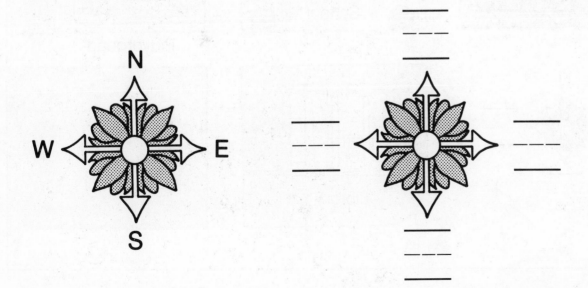

Using Cardinal Directions

WHAT I WILL LEARN

How do I use directions on a map?

Look at this map of Brookfield. You will use the
direction names on this map to find things.

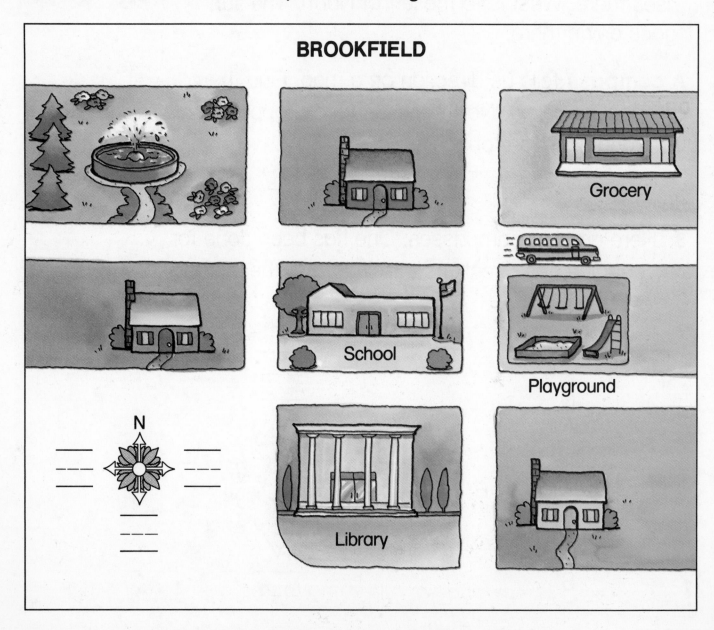

BROOKFIELD

PRINT IT

1. Find the compass on the map of Brookfield. Print the missing direction letters on the compass.

CIRCLE IT

2. Circle the playground in the EAST on the map.

3. Circle the house on the map that is just SOUTH of the playground.

4. Circle the house in the NORTH on the map.

DRAW A LINE

5. On the map, draw a line from the school to the playground.

6. Now, draw a line from the playground to the yellow house.

7. Now, draw a line from the yellow house to the library.

8. Now, draw a line from the library to the school.

9. What shape have you drawn? Draw it here.

What Are Map Symbols?

WHAT I WILL LEARN What are map **symbols**?
How do symbols help me read maps?

Here is a map of a farm.

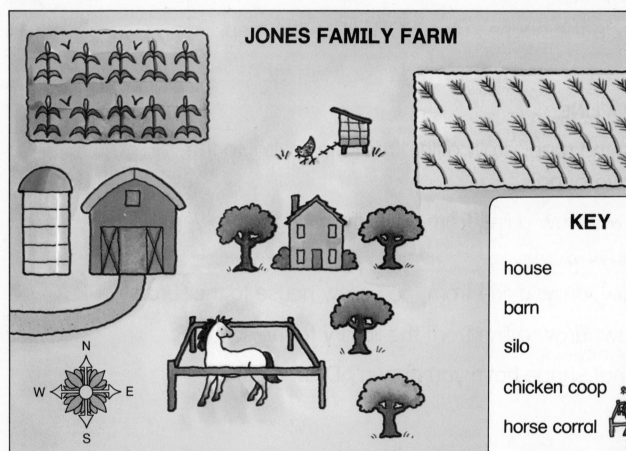

A **symbol** is a picture. It stands for a real thing.

This symbol 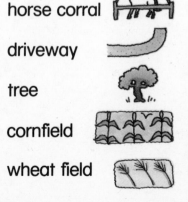 stands for a real tree.
Use this symbol to count the trees on the farm.

CIRCLE IT

1. Circle the symbol for the house in the key.

2. Circle the wheat field on the map.

3. What symbol on the map stands for silo?

4. How many wheat fields does the farm have?

   I   **2**   **3**

5. What is north of the 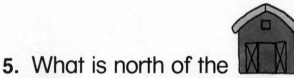 ?

DRAW A LINE

Here are some symbols with no words. Draw a line to match each symbol to the real thing.

6.   

7. 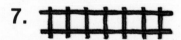   

8.   

Using a Map Key

WHAT I WILL LEARN Can I find places on a map?
How do I know what a map shows?

Here is a map and **key.**

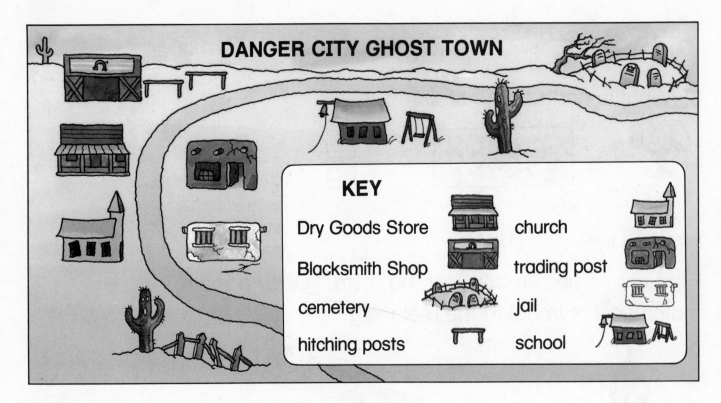

DANGER CITY GHOST TOWN

KEY

Dry Goods Store   church

Blacksmith Shop   trading post

cemetery   jail

hitching posts   school

CIRCLE IT

1. Which symbol stands for the church?

2. What is west of the jail?

Use this map and key to finish this page.

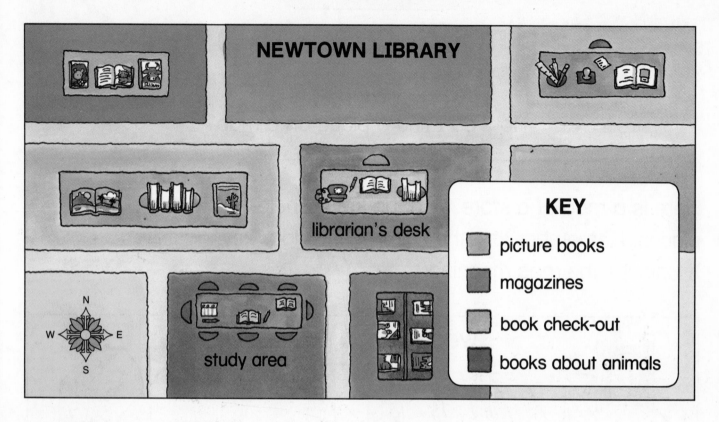

CIRCLE IT

3. What color is the area for books about animals?

   green   **orange**   **pink**

4. What color is the place just east of the study area?

   yellow   **red**   **blue**

COLOR IT

5. Color this ☐. Use the same color that shows
   where picture books are on the map.

6. Color this ☐. Use the same color that shows
   where magazines are on the map.

Finding Places with a Key

WHAT I WILL LEARN
How do I find a place on a map?

Here is a map of a store. Use the key to help you find places. Remember that the key is like a door key. It unlocks the map meaning.

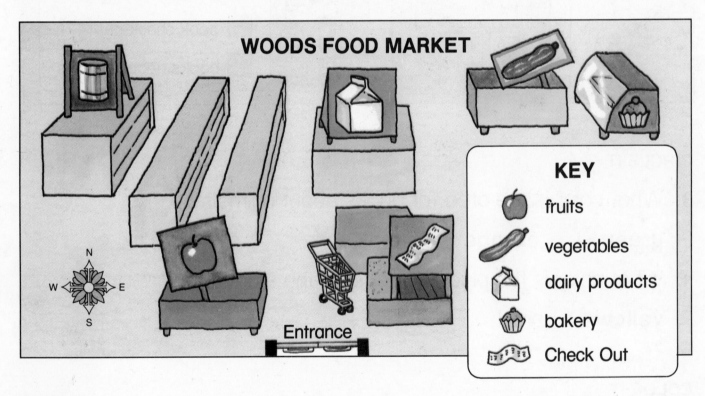

WOODS FOOD MARKET

KEY
- fruits
- vegetables
- dairy products
- bakery
- Check Out

Entrance

MARK IT

1. Put an ✗ on the food nearest the entrance.

2. Put a ✓ on the place to find vegetables.

3. Put an E on the place just east of the vegetables.

4. Put a ✓ on the Check Out counter.

Here is a treasure map.

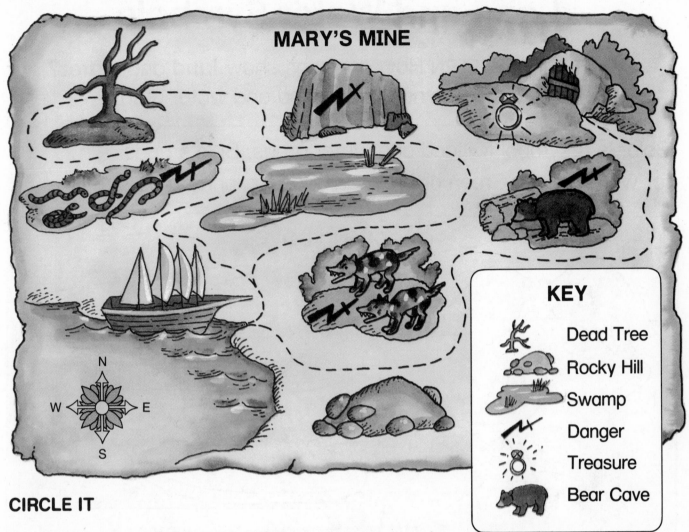

KEY

- Dead Tree
- Rocky Hill
- Swamp
- Danger
- Treasure
- Bear Cave

CIRCLE IT

5. Circle the thing north of the swamp on the map.

6. Circle the Rocky Hill on the map.

7. What is south of the Dead Tree?

   hill   **snakes**   **swamp**

8. Which one of these is a danger?

   wild dogs   **Dead Tree**   **Rocky Hill**

9. The treasure is marked by what symbol?

   X   **Treasure**

Land and Water Symbols

WHAT I WILL LEARN How do maps show **land** and **water?**
What are some names for land and water areas?

Color is a symbol for land and water areas. Blue stands
for water areas. Green or brown stands for land areas.

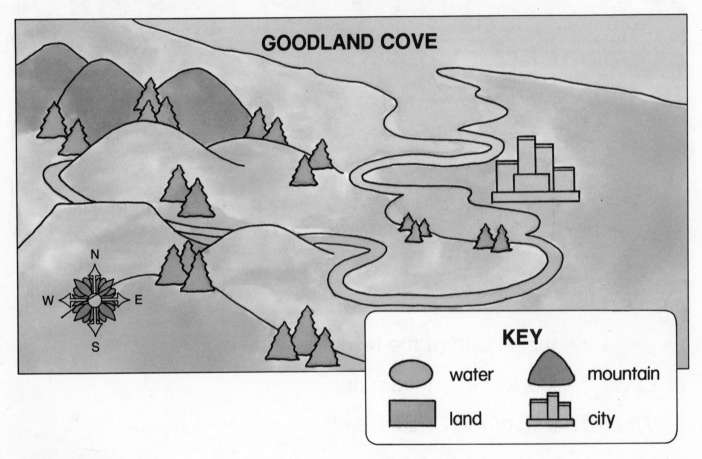

CIRCLE IT

1. What color shows water areas?   **blue**   **brown**

2. What water area is north of the city? Circle it on the map.

3. Find a lake on the map. Circle it.

4. Find a mountain on the map. Circle it.

Sometimes water areas look like this.

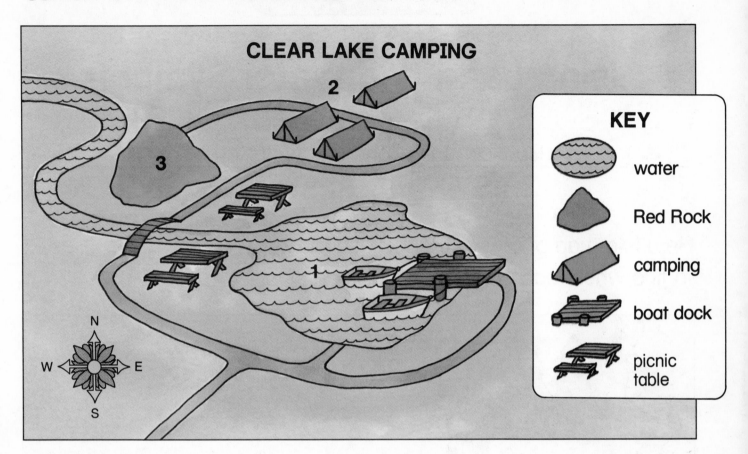

CLEAR LAKE CAMPING

KEY
- water
- Red Rock
- camping
- boat dock
- picnic table

CIRCLE IT

5. What symbol stands for water on this map?

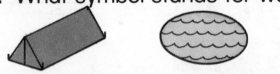

6. What number is on a water area?   I   **2**   **3**

7. Is the area west of Red Rock a land or water area?

   land   water

8. What is north of the lake?

   river   camping   boat dock

9. Go west from the boat dock. What do you come to first?

   showers   Red Rock   picnic table

Using Land and Water Symbols

WHAT I WILL LEARN

How can I find land and water areas?

Here is a map of a wildlife park. Use the key to find where each kind of animal lives.

DEER CREEK PARK

KEY

moose

deer

fox

wildcat

parking lot

river

CIRCLE IT

1. What color on the map shows water?

   blue　　　**yellow**　　　**green**

2. What does this symbol 〰 stand for?

   a mountain　　　**a river**　　　**a field**

3. Circle the lot on the map where cars are parked.

4. Beavers usually live near water. The park plans to add a beaver family. Which number on the map shows the best home for beavers?

   1　　　**2**　　　**3**

5. If you went west from the parking lot, what animal would you see first?

   deer　　　**moose**　　　**wildcat**

DRAW IT

6. On the map, draw a line NORTH from where the moose live to the fox den.

7. Draw a box around where the wildcat lives.

8. Draw a fence ∧∧∧ to keep the deer out of the place where the moose are.

Following Directions and Tracing Paths on a Map

WHAT I WILL LEARN Can I draw a **path** on a map?
Can I follow directions on a map to answer questions?

Here is a map of an **imaginary** place. Read carefully
and follow the directions. You will draw two **paths.**

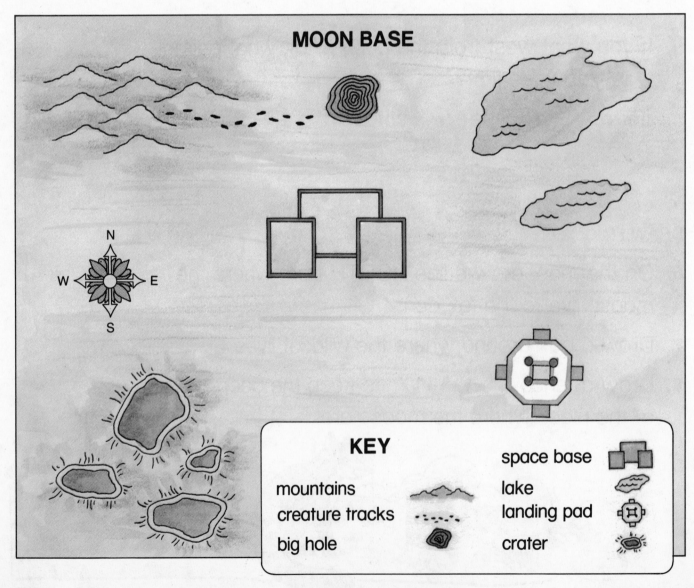

MOON BASE

KEY

mountains

creature tracks

big hole

space base

lake

landing pad

crater

DRAW IT

1. Draw a path like this ----------- as you follow the directions.

    a. Draw the path NORTH from the Landing Pad to the little lake.

    b. Next, draw the path WEST to the Space Base.

    c. Now, draw the path NORTH to Big Hole.

    d. Follow the creature tracks WEST.

PRINT IT

2. Where did you end up?

_____

- -

_____

DRAW IT

3. Draw a path like this ▬▬▬▬▬▬▬.
Follow these directions.

    a. Start at the big lake. Draw the path SOUTH to the little lake.

    b. Now, draw the path WEST to the Space Base.

    c. Now draw the path to the craters.

CIRCLE IT

4. In which direction did you draw your last path?

North   **South**   **East**   **West**

More Tracing Paths on a Map

WHAT I WILL LEARN Can I find where to go on a map?
Can I follow a path on a map?

Look at the map on this page.

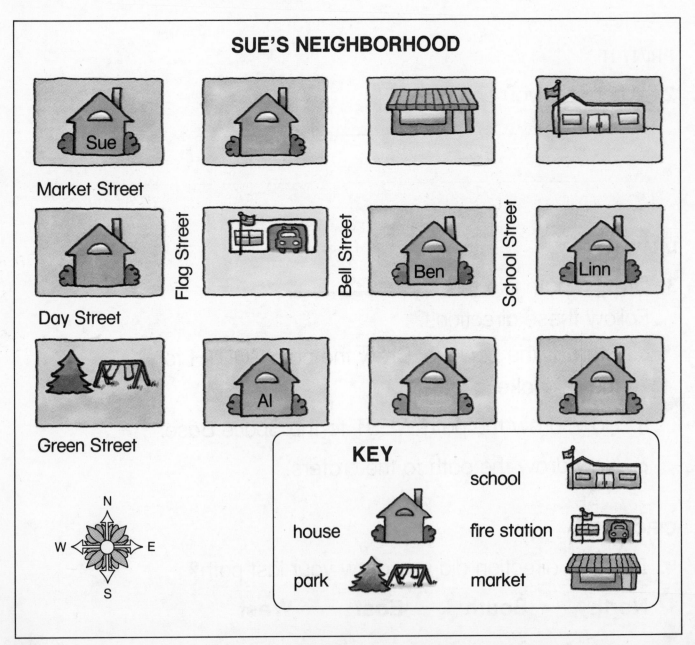

SUE'S NEIGHBORHOOD

Market Street

Day Street

Green Street

Flag Street

Bell Street

School Street

Sue

Ben

Linn

Al

N W E S

KEY

house

park

school

fire station

market

CIRCLE IT

1. What does this [symbol] stand for?

   school   **fire station**   **house**

2. What does this [symbol] stand for?

   market   **house**   **school**

DRAW IT

3. Find Al's house. Find Linn's house. Draw the path Al would take to visit Ben and then go to Linn's house. Color the path brown.

4. Find the Market. Draw the path Sue would take if she went from her home to the Market. Color the path green.

5. Draw a red line from Al's house to the Park. Al will go on Green Street.

6. Draw a blue line from Ben's house to the School.

CIRCLE IT

7. What street do Ben and Linn cross to get to the School?

   School Street   **Market Street**   **Flag Street**

8. What street goes by Sue's house and Al's house?

   School Street   **Flag Street**   **Day Street**

Distance Words

WHAT I WILL LEARN What do these words mean:
near, far, longer, shorter, closest, and **farthest**?
Can I find the shortest way?

Distance means how far or how long.
The girl walked **one step.**

Far is a long distance.
Near is a short distance.

Some distances are **longer.**
Some are **shorter.**

MATCH IT

1. Draw a line from the word to its picture.

near

far

longer

shorter

Look at this map.

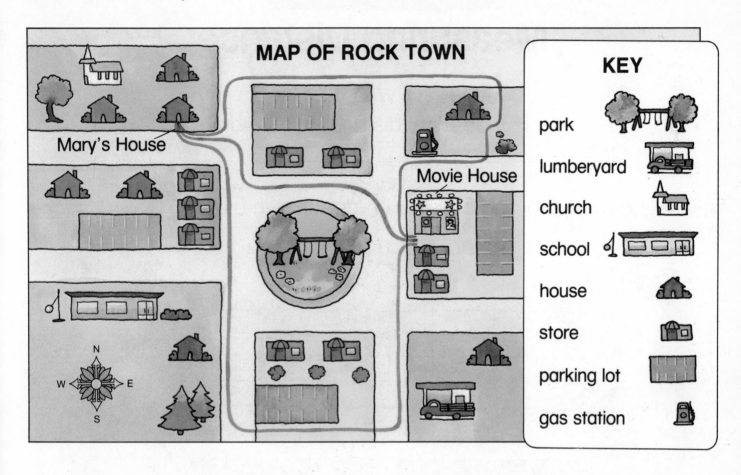

MAP OF ROCK TOWN

Mary's House

Movie House

KEY

park

lumberyard

church

school

house

store

parking lot

gas station

The stores are **closest** to the park. The lumberyard is
farthest from the church.

CIRCLE IT

2. What is near the gas station?

   church   **school**   **house**

3. What is closest to the school?

   church   **parking lot**   **gas station**

4. There are three colored lines on the map. Which shows
   the **shortest** way from Mary's house to the Movie
   House?

   red line   **green line**   **blue line**

Measuring Distance

WHAT I WILL LEARN
How do I find distance on a map?

Here is a map showing how **far** children ran in a race.

BELL SCHOOL RACE

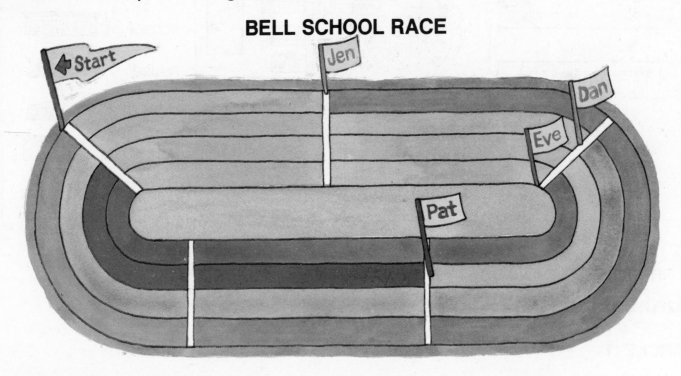

The children put their names on the blocks where they stopped. Count the blocks to see how far the children ran. Dan ran three blocks.

CIRCLE IT

1. Who ran the shortest distance? **Dan**   **Pat**

2. Who ran the longest distance? **Jen**   **Eve**

3. How far did Pat run? **3 blocks**   **4 blocks**   **2 blocks**

The children are playing a game. To play this game,
you go from Start to End.

RACE BOARD GAME

Paths on this game have different **distances.**

CIRCLE IT

4. What is the very shortest path from Start to End?

    red　　　**blue**　　　**green**

5. How many spaces is it from Start to End on the
   green path?　　　**10**　　　**17**　　　**20**

6. How many spaces is it from the Danger space to the
   Safe space?　　　**4**　　　**7**　　　**9**

Comparing Distance

WHAT I WILL LEARN

Can I find the shortest distance on a map?

Can I learn when a distance is long or short?

Look at the map of the State Fair on the next page.
Use it to help you finish this page.

CIRCLE IT

1. How many sidewalk squares are between Square I
   and Square A on the map?

   I   **3**   **5**

2. Circle the Ticket Booth on the map.

3. Circle the Science Building on the map.

DRAW IT

4. What is the shortest distance from Square A to
   Square D? Draw that path on the map in red.

5. What is the longest distance from Square I to
   Square 3? Draw that path on the map in blue.

6. Draw the shortest distance from Square B to
   Square C in green.

STATE FAIR

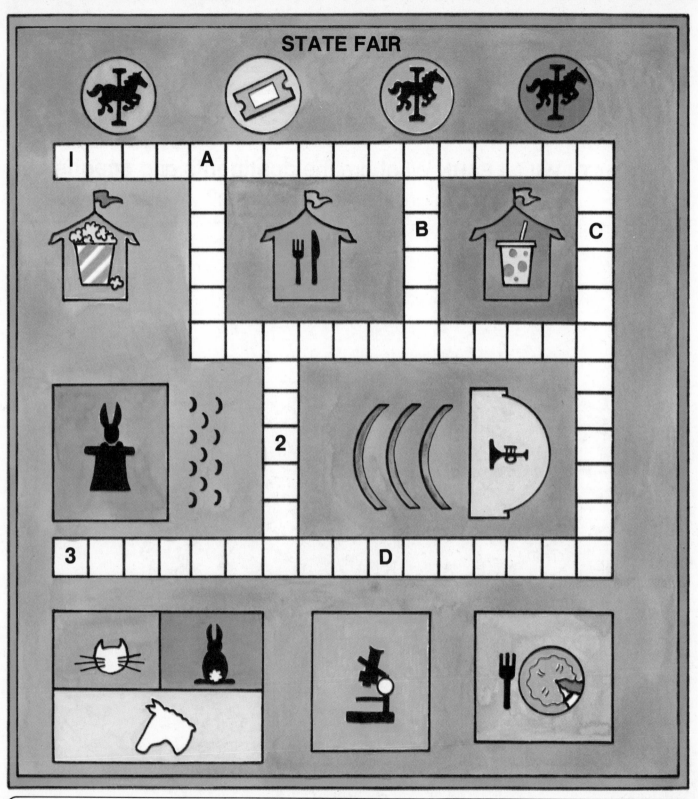

KEY

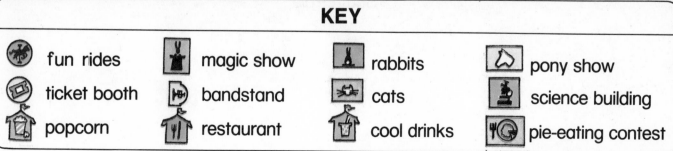

- fun rides
- ticket booth
- popcorn
- magic show
- bandstand
- restaurant
- rabbits
- cats
- cool drinks
- pony show
- science building
- pie-eating contest

Finding Real Places on Earth

WHAT I WILL LEARN What are the **continents** and **oceans**? Where are they on our Earth?

THE EARTH

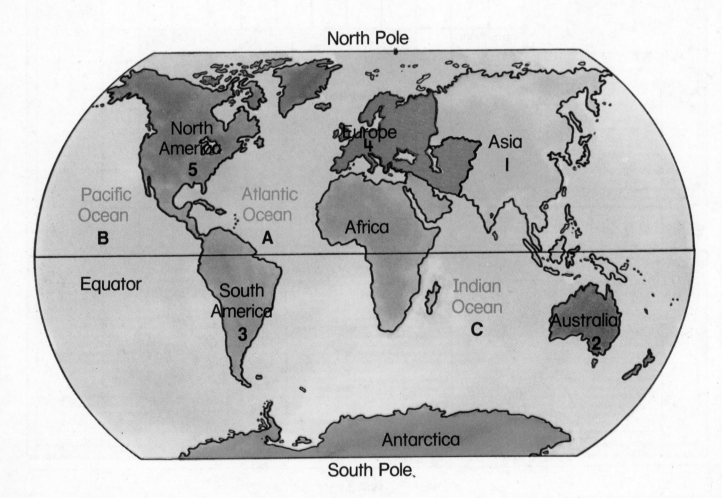

Find the blue printed words on the map. These words name **oceans.** An ocean is a very large body of water.

CIRCLE IT

1. Find and circle the North Pole.

2. Find and circle the South Pole.

3. Is the North Pole a land or water body?

   land　　　　**water**

4. What is the largest land body on the map?

   A　　　　**B**　　　　**I**　　　　**2**

5. What is the place marked **2** on the map?

   land　　　　**water**

Find the black words. These words name **continents.** A continent is a very large body of land.

PRINT IT

6. Africa is a body of _____.

   　　　　　　　　　　land　　　**water**

7. Find the continent Asia. What number is on it?

   Print it here. _____

8. Find the continent North America. What number is on it?

   Print its number here. _____

Finding Places Near Me

WHAT I WILL LEARN Where do I live?
What are some places in my **country?**

The **United States** is a country in North America. The map on page 39 shows places in the United States.

Use the map to help you finish this page.

CIRCLE IT

1. What is the name of your country? Circle it.
   United States   **Canada**   **Mexico**

2. What large river runs through the United States?
   Superior   **Mississippi**   **Atlantic**

3. What city is the farthest west on this map?
   San Francisco   **New York**   **Houston**

4. What city is farthest east on this map?
   San Francisco   **New York**   **Chicago**

COLOR IT

5. Find your state on the map. Color it red.

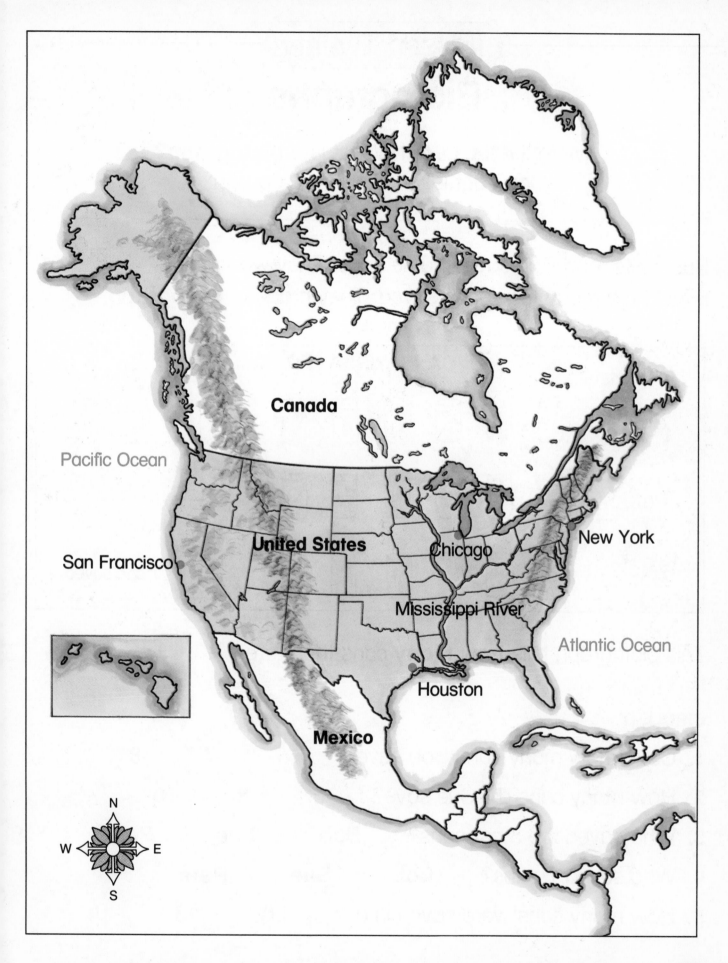

Pacific Ocean

Canada

United States

San Francisco

Chicago

New York

Mississippi River

Atlantic Ocean

Houston

Mexico

N
W ← → E
S

Pictographs

WHAT I WILL LEARN What is a **pictograph?**
Can I get ideas from a pictograph?

Sue, Pete, and Bob saved some cans. They wanted to know how many they each saved. They made a **pictograph.**

This pictograph tells **how many** cans there are.

CIRCLE IT

1. Count how many cans Bob saved.   6   7   8

2. How many cans did Sue save?   6   8   10

3. Who saved the most cans?   **Bob**   **Sue**   **Pete**

4. Who saved 7 cans?   **Bob**   **Sue**   **Pete**

5. How many cans were saved in all?   **20**   **23**   14

Here is another pictograph. It tells **what kinds** of pets the First Grade Class has.

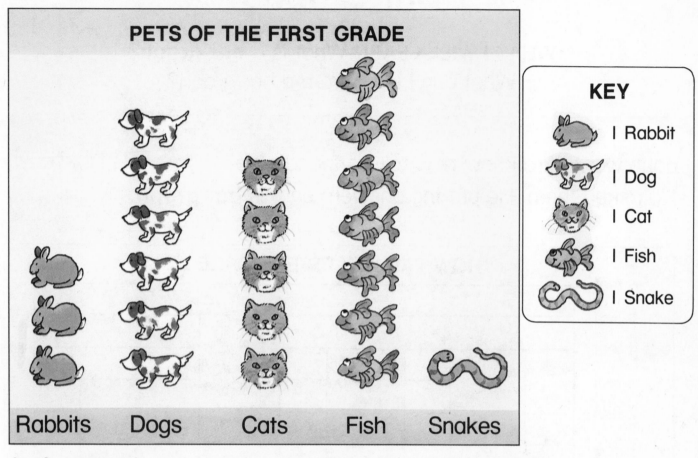

A **pictograph** can answer questions. It is easy to read.

CIRCLE IT

6. What kind of pet do most children have?

       dog   **cat**   **fish**

7. How many rabbits does the class have?   **3**   **5**   **7**

8. How many fish does the class have?   **5**   **6**   **7**

9. How many snakes does the class have?   **I**   **2**   **3**

Bar Graphs

WHAT I WILL LEARN What is a **bar graph**?
What can I learn from a bar graph?

John wanted to know how tall his friends are.
He asked them. He put the answers on this **bar graph.**

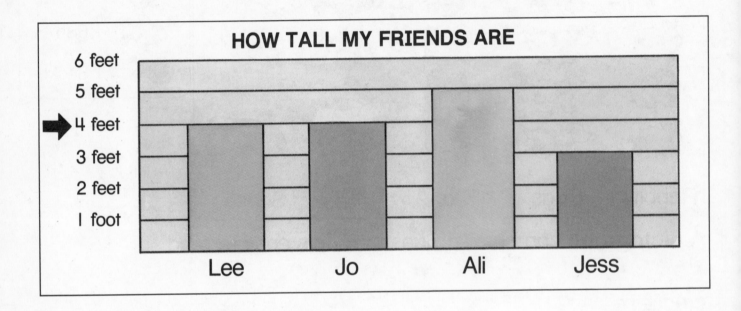

A **bar graph** is easy to read. Find Jo's name.
Go to the top of the bar. Find the arrow on the side.
That shows Jo is 4 feet tall.

CIRCLE IT

1. How tall is Ali?   **3 feet**   **4 feet**   **5 feet**

2. Who is tallest?   **Lee**   **Ali**

3. Who is shortest?   **Jess**   **Ali**

Here is another **bar graph.** It has colored bars. It shows **how far** some children rode bikes.

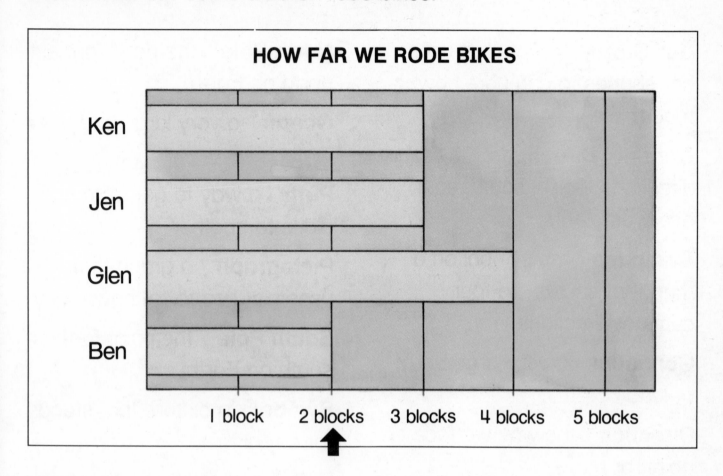

HOW FAR WE RODE BIKES

Ken

Jen

Glen

Ben

| 1 block | 2 blocks | 3 blocks | 4 blocks | 5 blocks |

Find Ben's name. Go to the end of his bar. Look for the arrow on the bottom. That shows Ben rode 2 blocks.

CIRCLE IT

4. Who rode the greatest number of blocks?

    Ken   **Glen**

5. Who rode the smallest number of blocks?

    Jen   **Ben**

6. What two children rode the same distance?

    Ken and Jen   **Glen and Ben**

Bar Graph graph that uses bar shapes to compare how much

Cardinal Directions the four directions, north, south, east and west

Compass the symbol on a map that shows the four cardinal directions

Continent a very large body of land

Direction the way we face, point, or move

Distance how far one place is from another

Map Key a list of symbols on a map, and what they mean

Map a drawing of a place that uses pictures to stand for real things

North Pole the point farthest north on Earth

Ocean a very large body of water

Path a way to get from one place to another

Pictograph a graph that uses pictures to tell how many

South Pole the point farthest south on Earth

Symbol a picture that stands for a real thing

Title a name that tells what a map or picture is about

Answer Key

Lesson One

1. a zoo
2. eating
3. 2
4. (child on page 3 circled)
5. 4
6. 6
7. (balloons colored green)
8. (ice cream cones colored yellow)

Lesson Two

1. a classroom
2. ("MRS. MOE'S CLASSROOM" circled)
3. a classroom
4. ("A MAP OF MRS. MOE'S CLASSROOM" circled)
5. (paint table circled)
6. (Mrs. Moe's desk colored brown)

Lesson Three

1,2,3.

MARIA'S BACKYARD

4. a place

5,6.

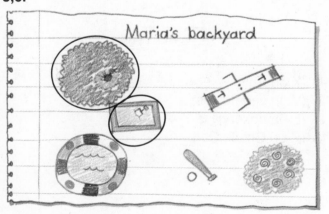

Maria's backyard

7. a place

Lesson Four

1,2,3,4.

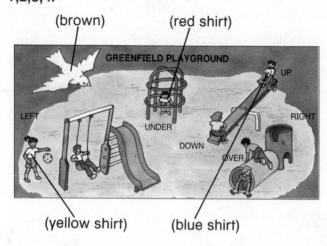

(brown)   (red shirt)

GREENFIELD PLAYGROUND

LEFT   UNDER   DOWN   OVER   UP   RIGHT

(yellow shirt)   (blue shirt)

5. right
6. down
7. left
8. over

Lesson Five

1. turtle
2. backward
3. away from
4. bed
5. forward
6. (shoe circled)
7. (bat circled)
8. (line drawn between red books)
9. (arrow drawn from door to window)

1. (North Pole circled)   2. (South Pole circled)
3.

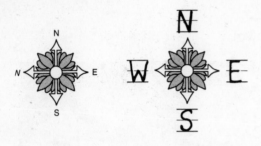

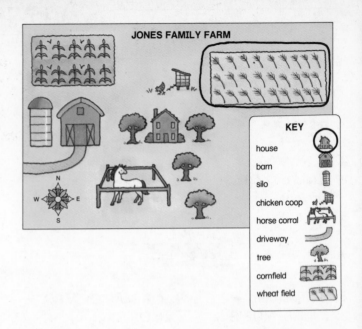

JONES FAMILY FARM

KEY

house
barn
silo
chicken coop
horse corral
driveway
tree
cornfield
wheat field

Lesson Seven

1-8.

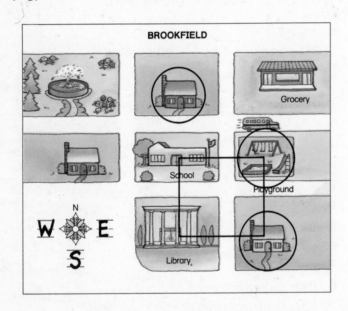

9. ☐ (square)

3. (silo)   5. (cornfield)
4. I
6,7,8.

Lesson Eight

1. (house in KEY circled)
2. (wheat field circled)

Lesson Nine

1. (church)   5. (pink)
2. (church)   6. (red)
3. green
4. red

Lesson Ten

1. (X on fruit)
2. (V on vegetables)
3. (E on bakery)
4. (✓ on Check Out)

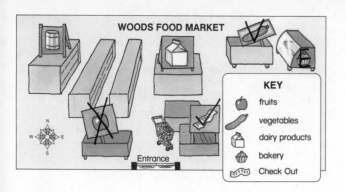

WOODS FOOD MARKET

5,6.

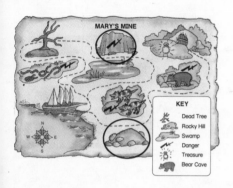

7. snakes

8. wild dogs

9. (symbol for treasure)

Lesson Eleven

1. blue

2,3,4.

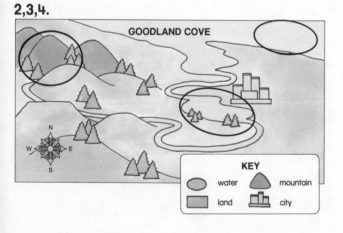

5. (water symbol)

6. 1

7. water

8. camping area

9. picnic table

Lesson Twelve

1. blue

2. a river

3,6,7,8.

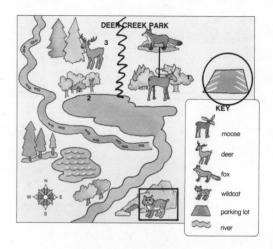

4. 2

5. moose

Lesson Thirteen

1,3.

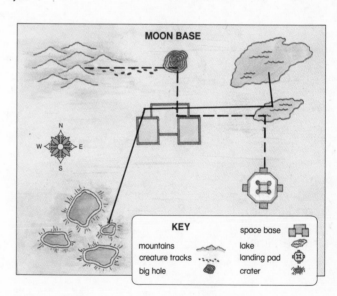

2. mountains

4. South

Lesson Fourteen

1. fire station

2. house

3-6.

SUE'S NEIGHBORHOOD

(green) (blue)

(brown)

(red)

7. Market Street   **8.** Flag Street

I. 3.   2-6.

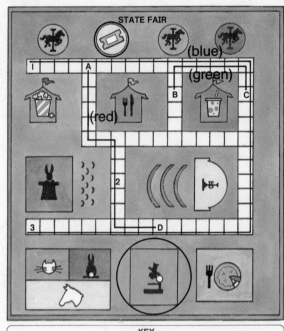

Lesson Fifteen

I.

near
far
longer
shorter

2. house

3. parking lot

4. green line

Lesson Sixteen

1. Pat
2. Jen
3. 2 blocks
4. blue
5. 17
6. 4

Lesson Eighteen

1. (North Pole circled)   5. land
2. (South Pole circled)   6. land
3. water   7. I
4. I   8. 5

Lesson Nineteen

1. United States   4. New York
2. Mississippi   5. Answers will vary.
3. San Francisco

Lesson Twenty

1. 6   4. Pete   7. 3
2. 10   5. 23   8. 7
3. Sue   6. Fish   9. I

Lesson Twenty-One

1. 5 feet   3. Jess   5. Ben
2. Ali   4. Glen   6. Ken and Jen